Not in Need of Rescue

A Coloring Book of Women in Fantasy Settings

by author/artist
M.C.A. Hogarth

STUDIO
MCAH

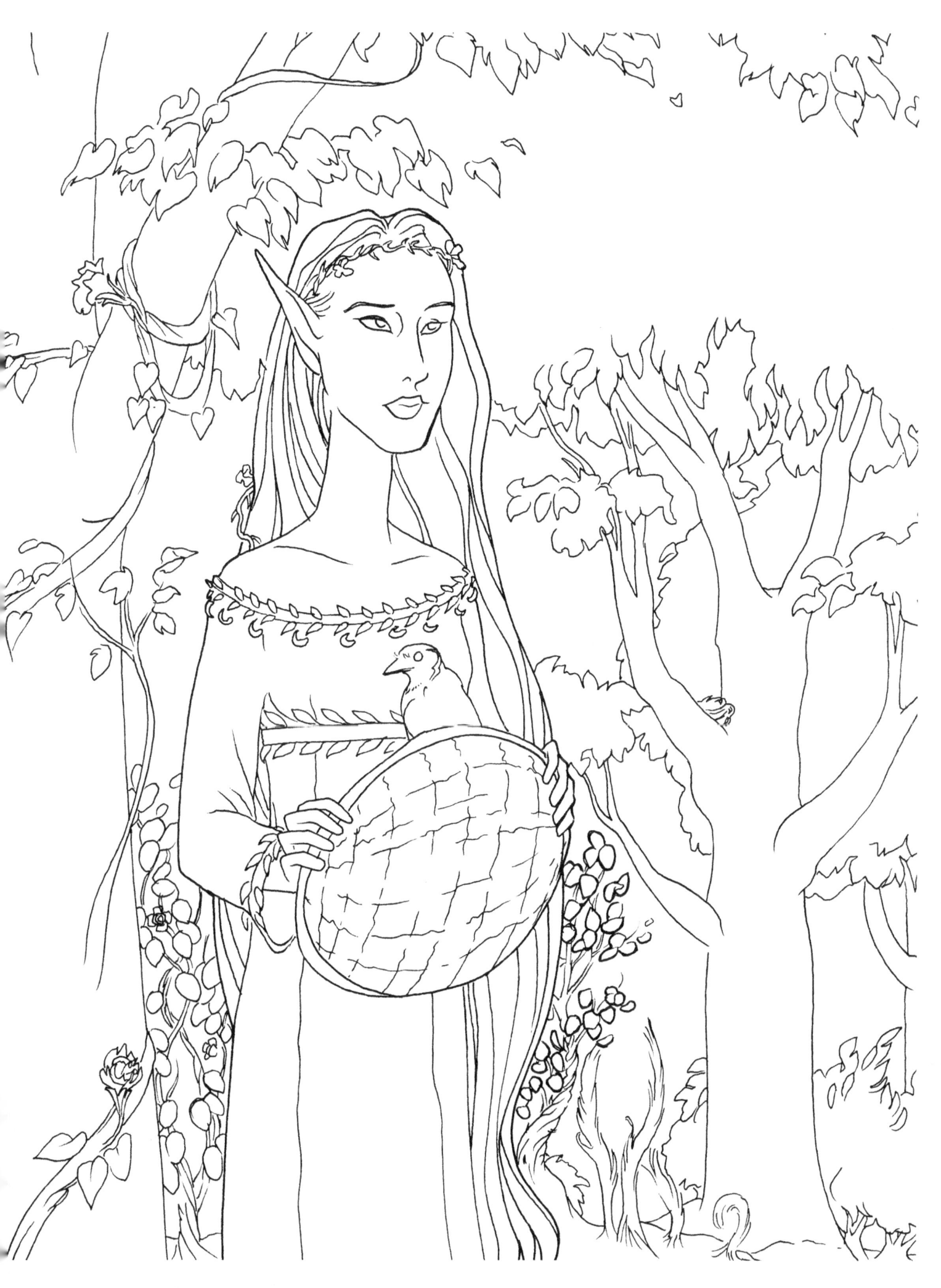

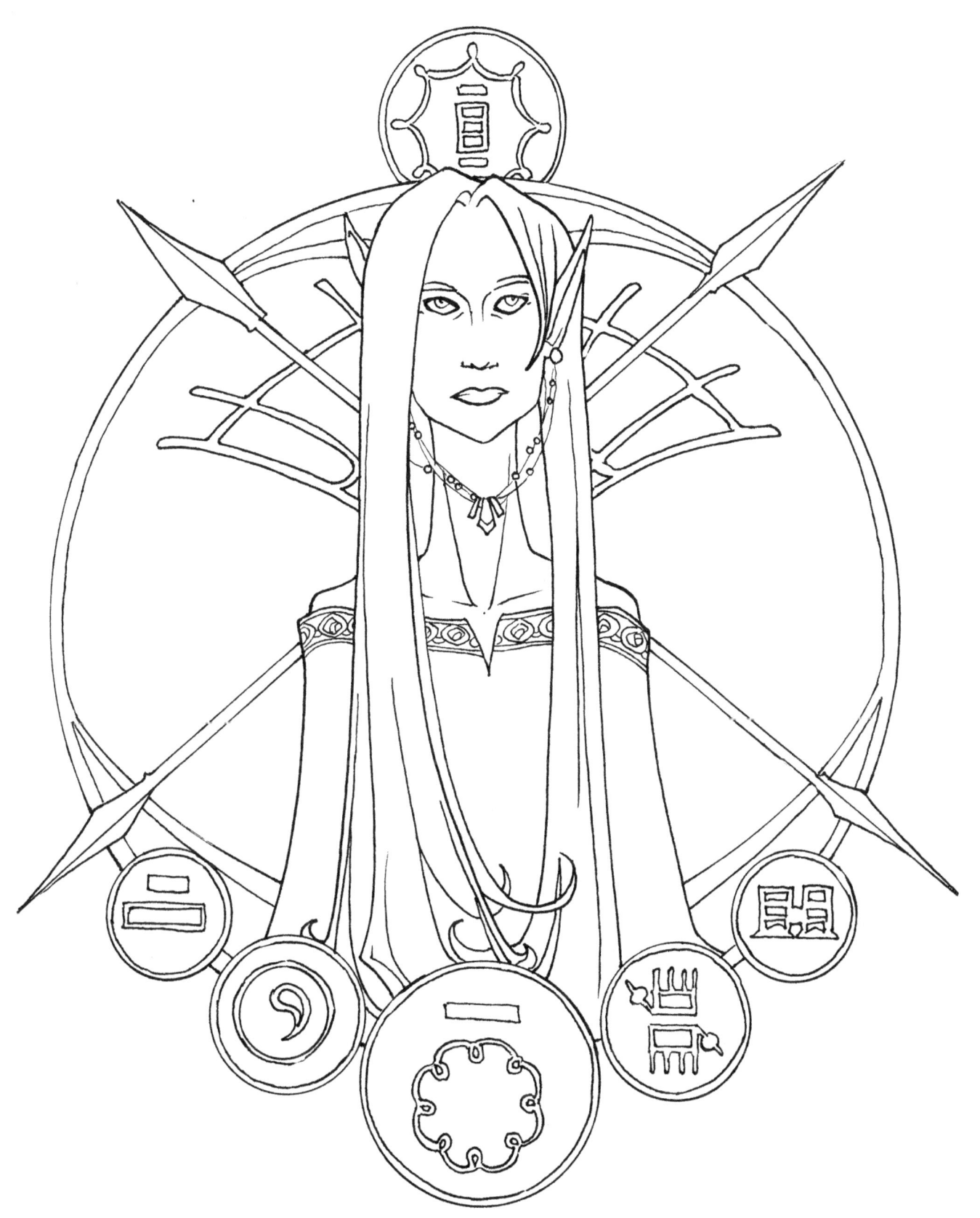

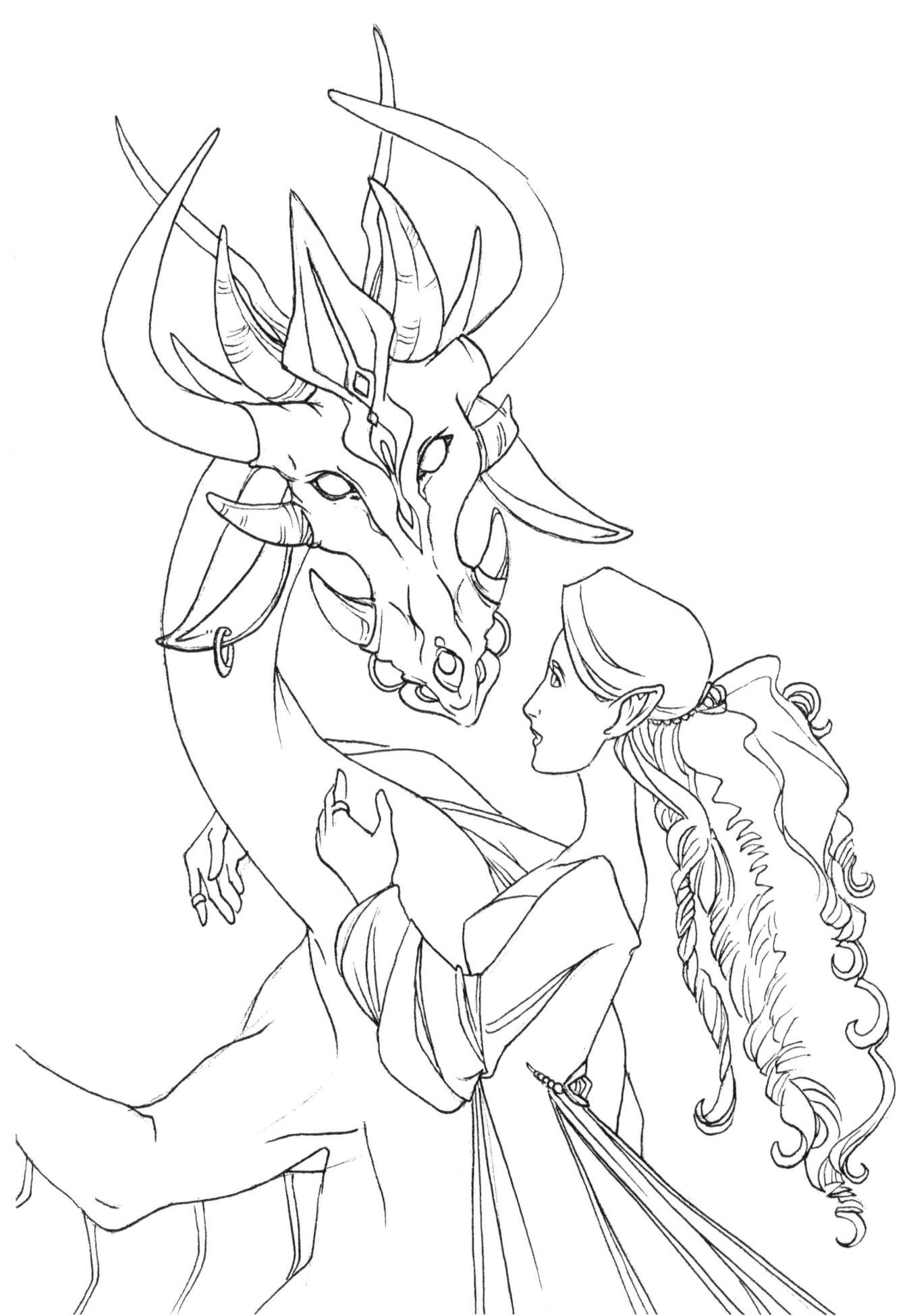

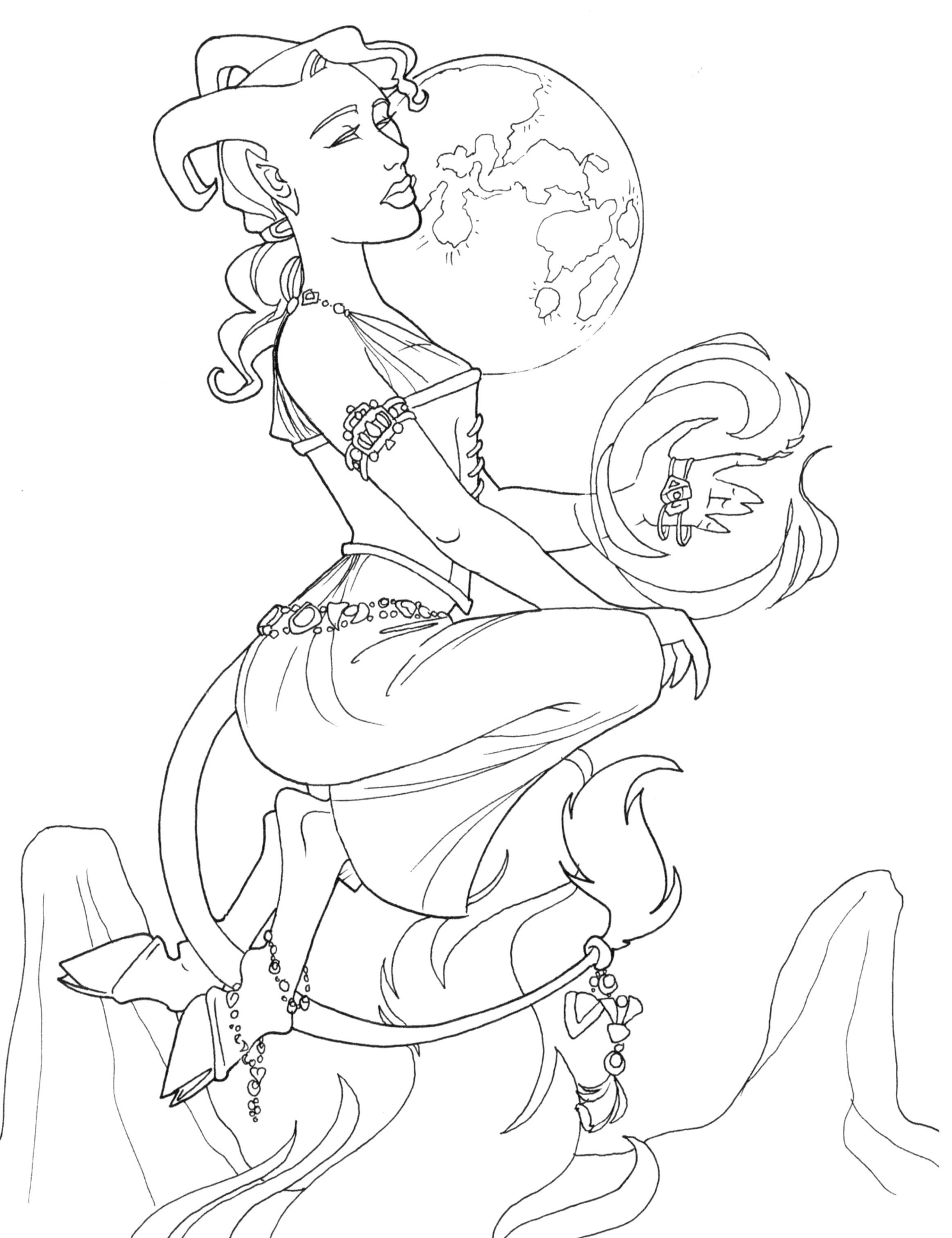

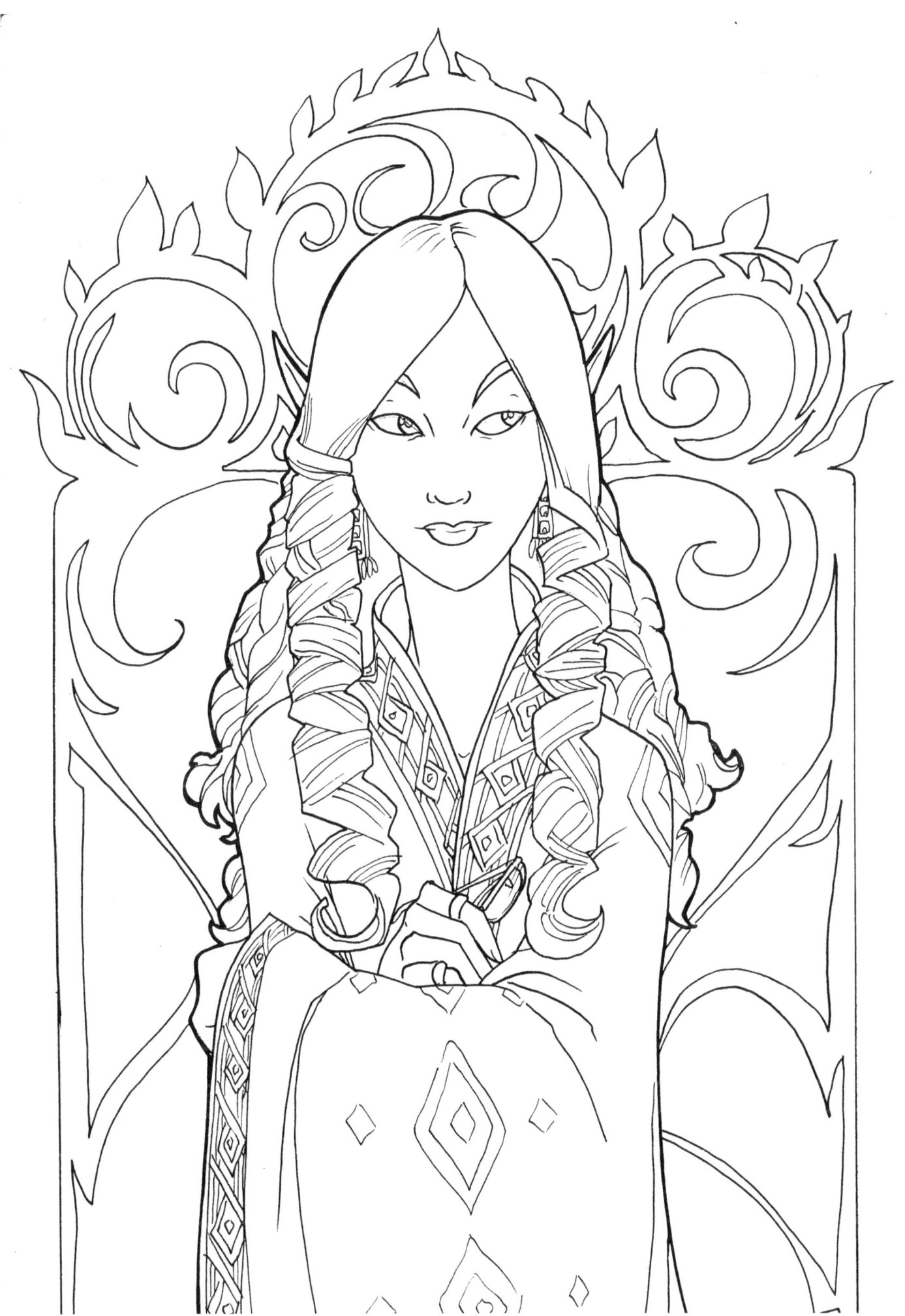

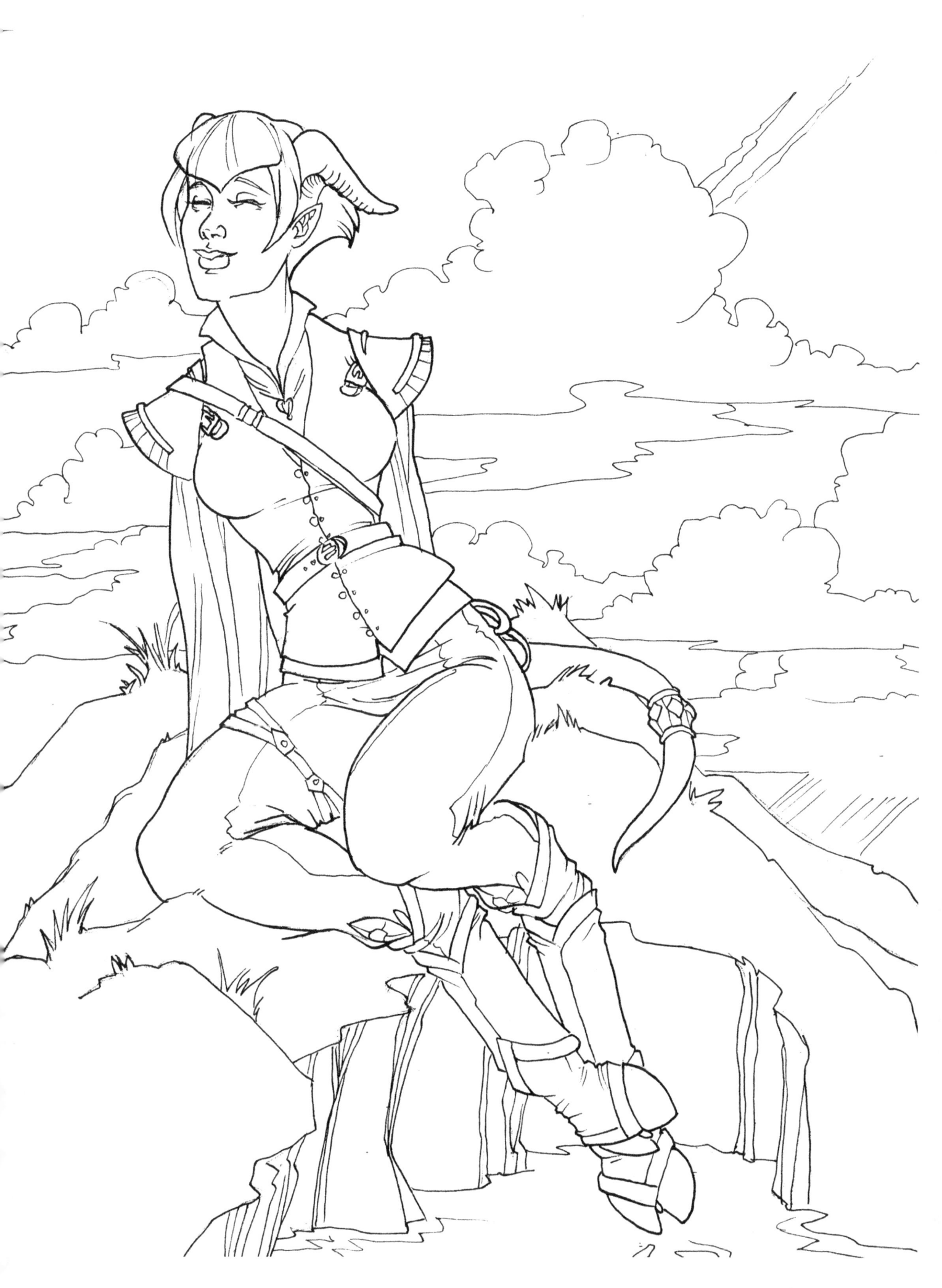

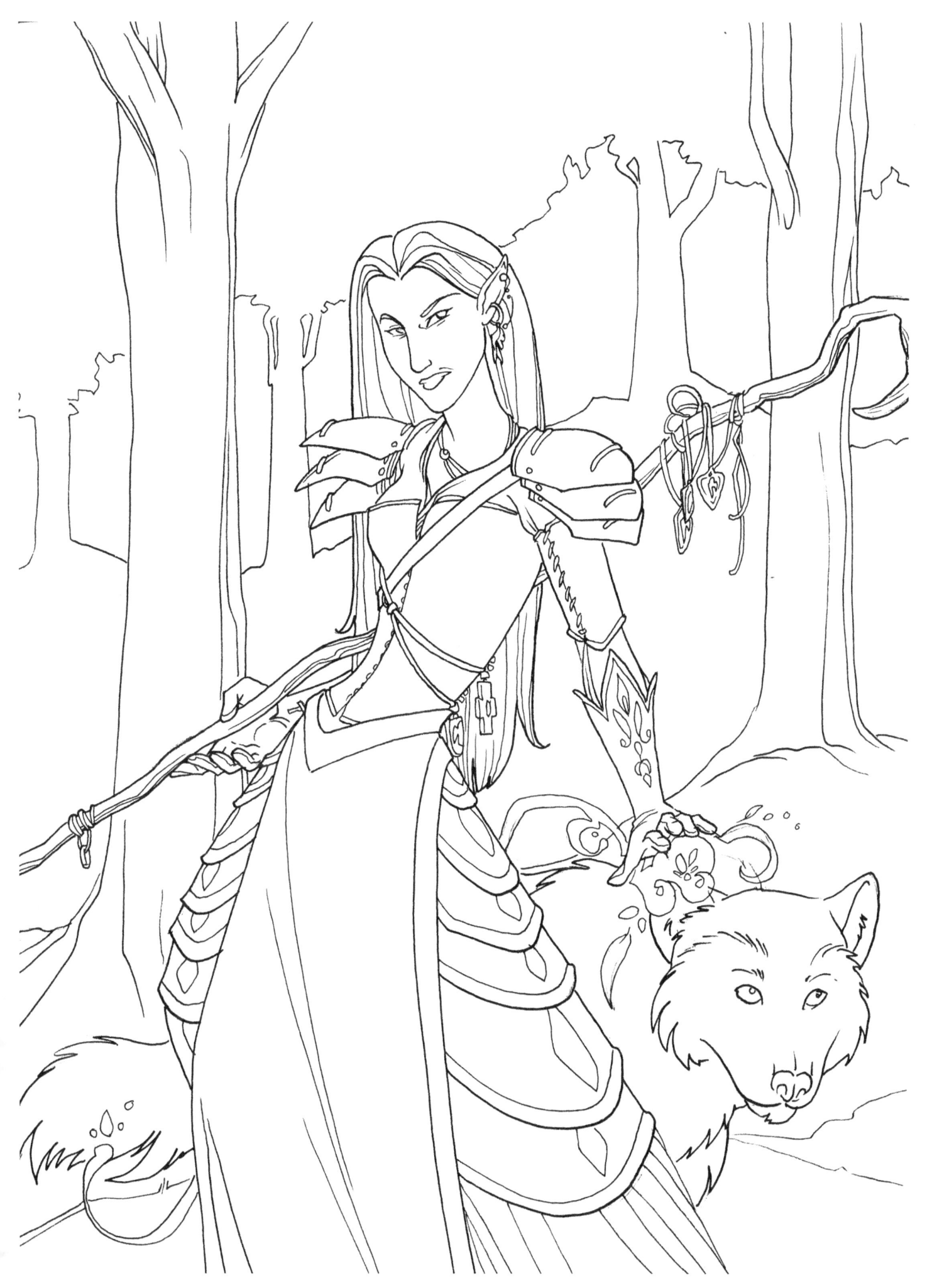

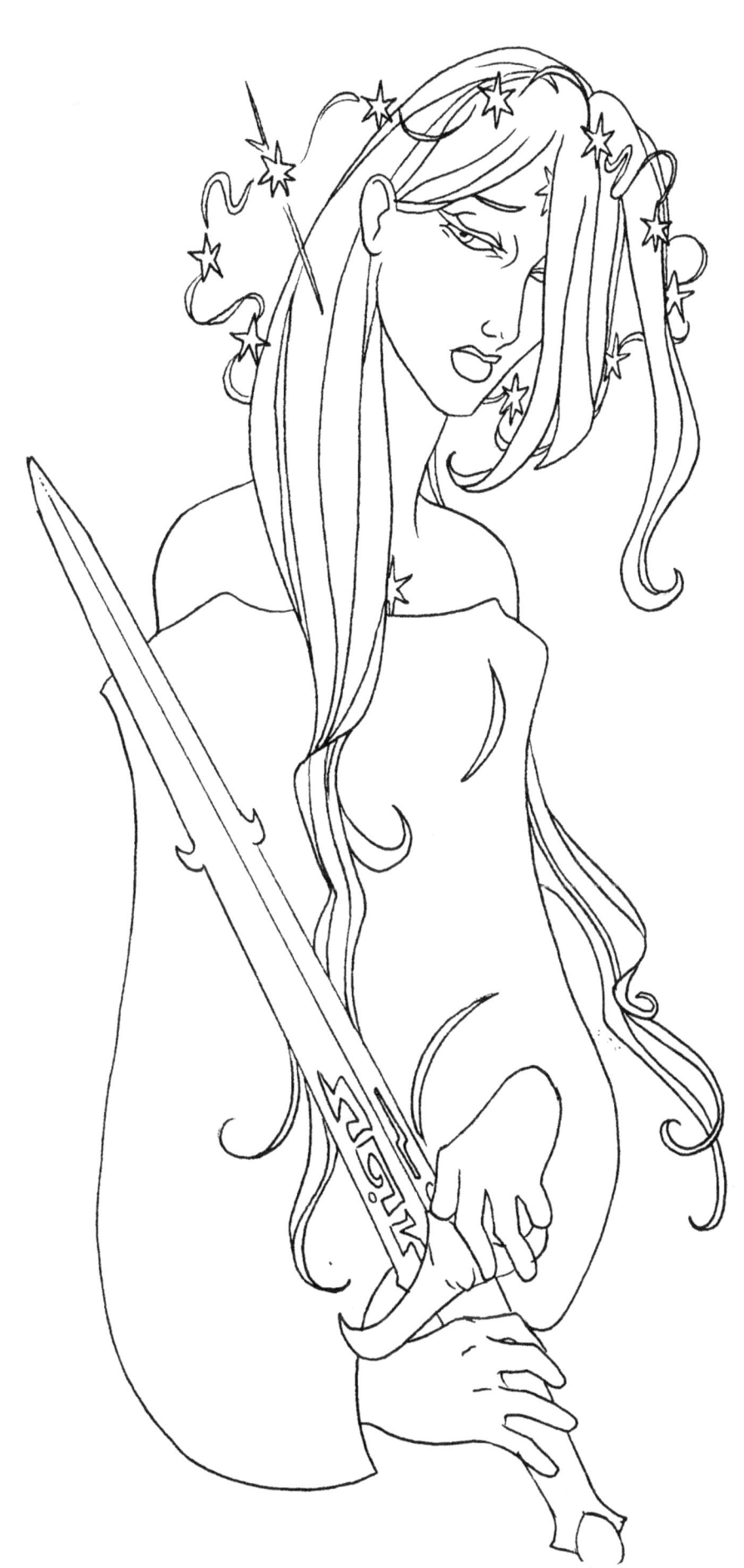

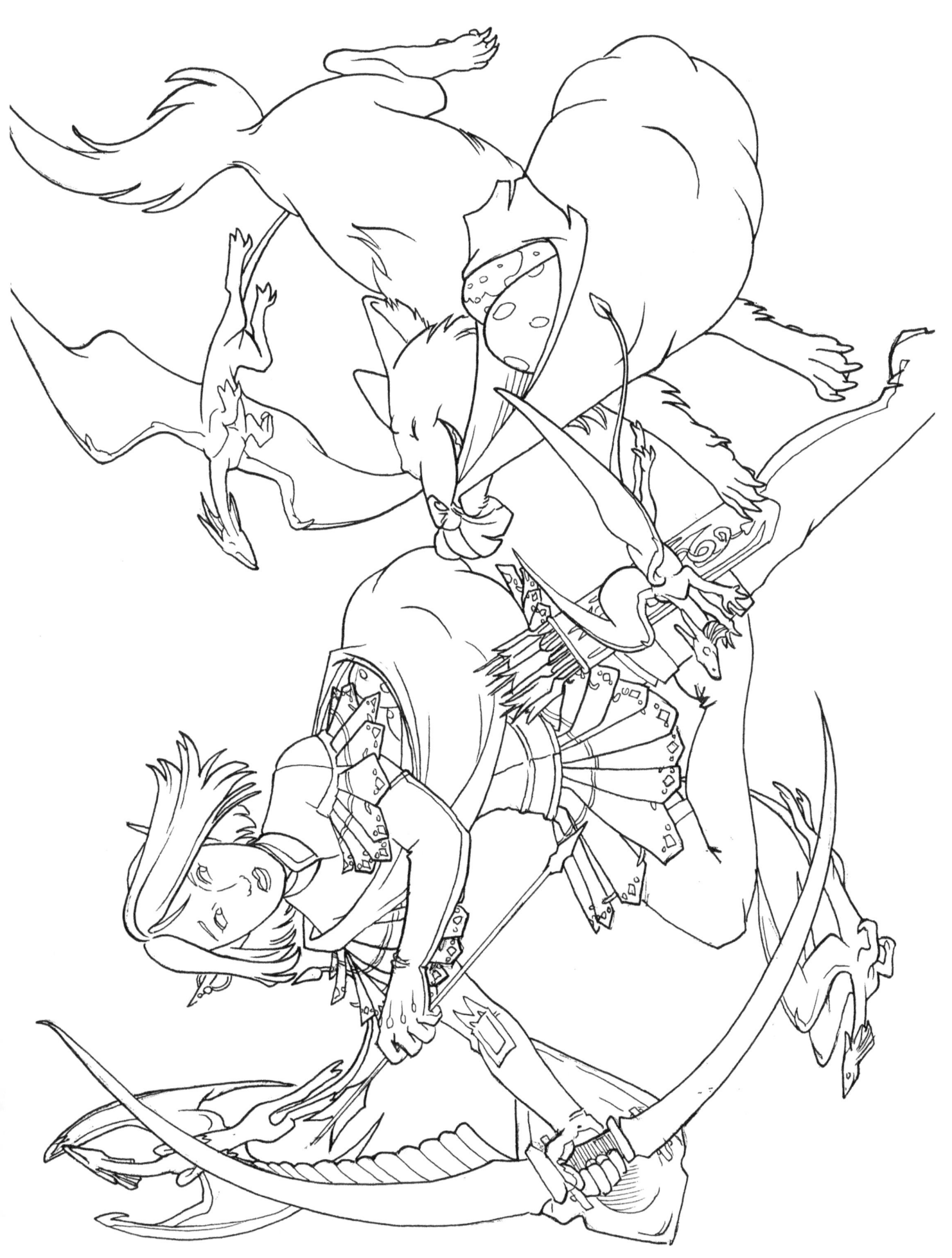

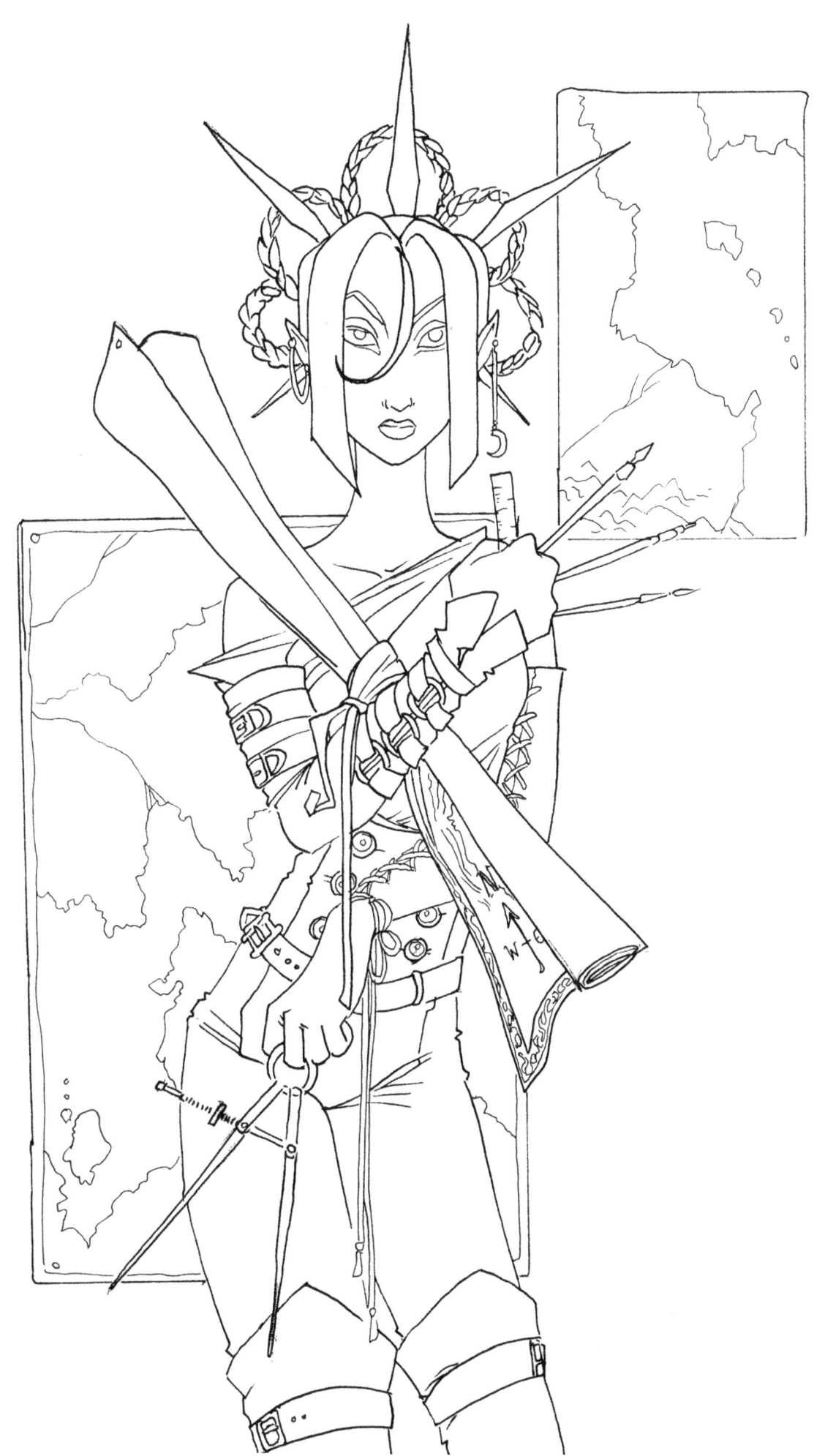

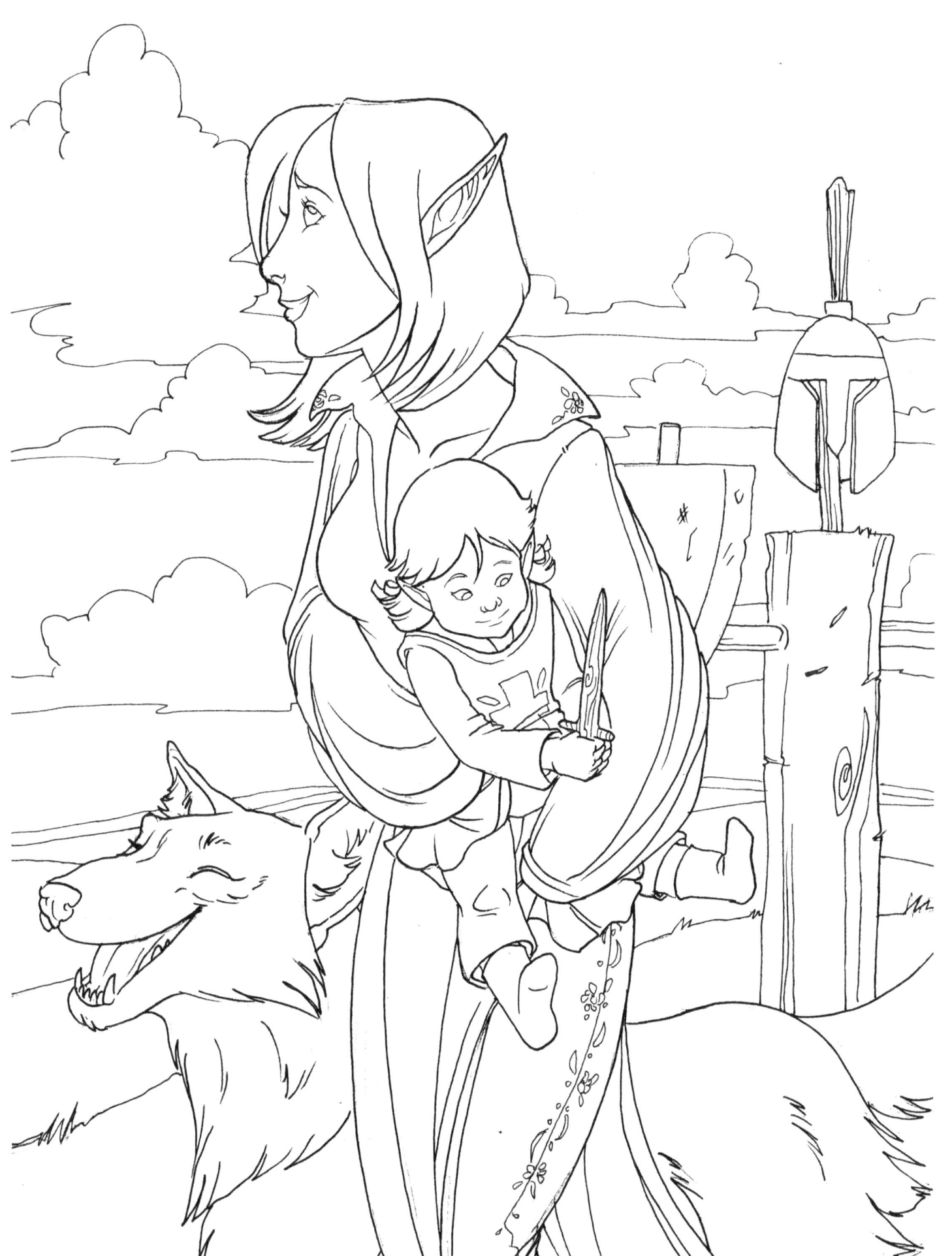

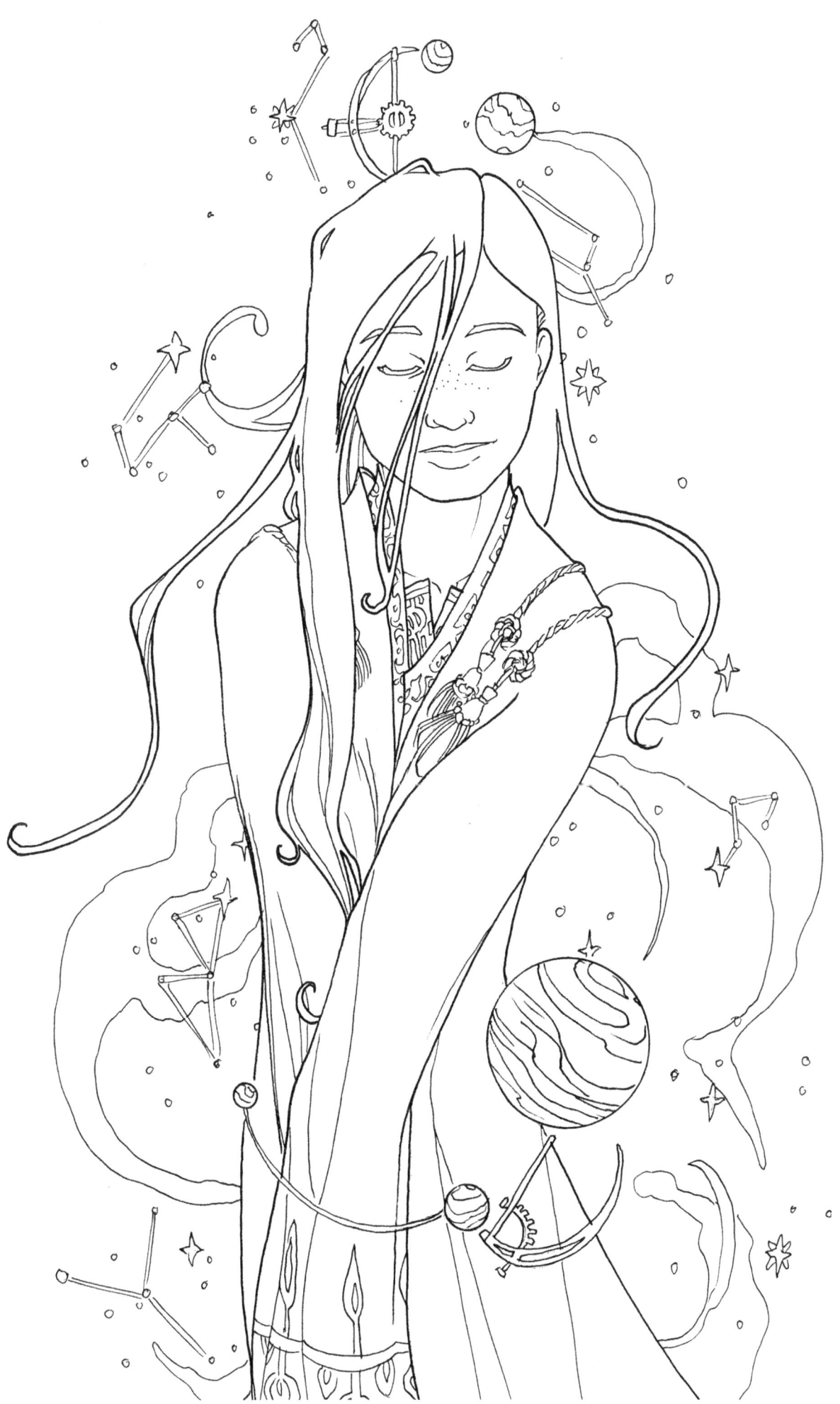

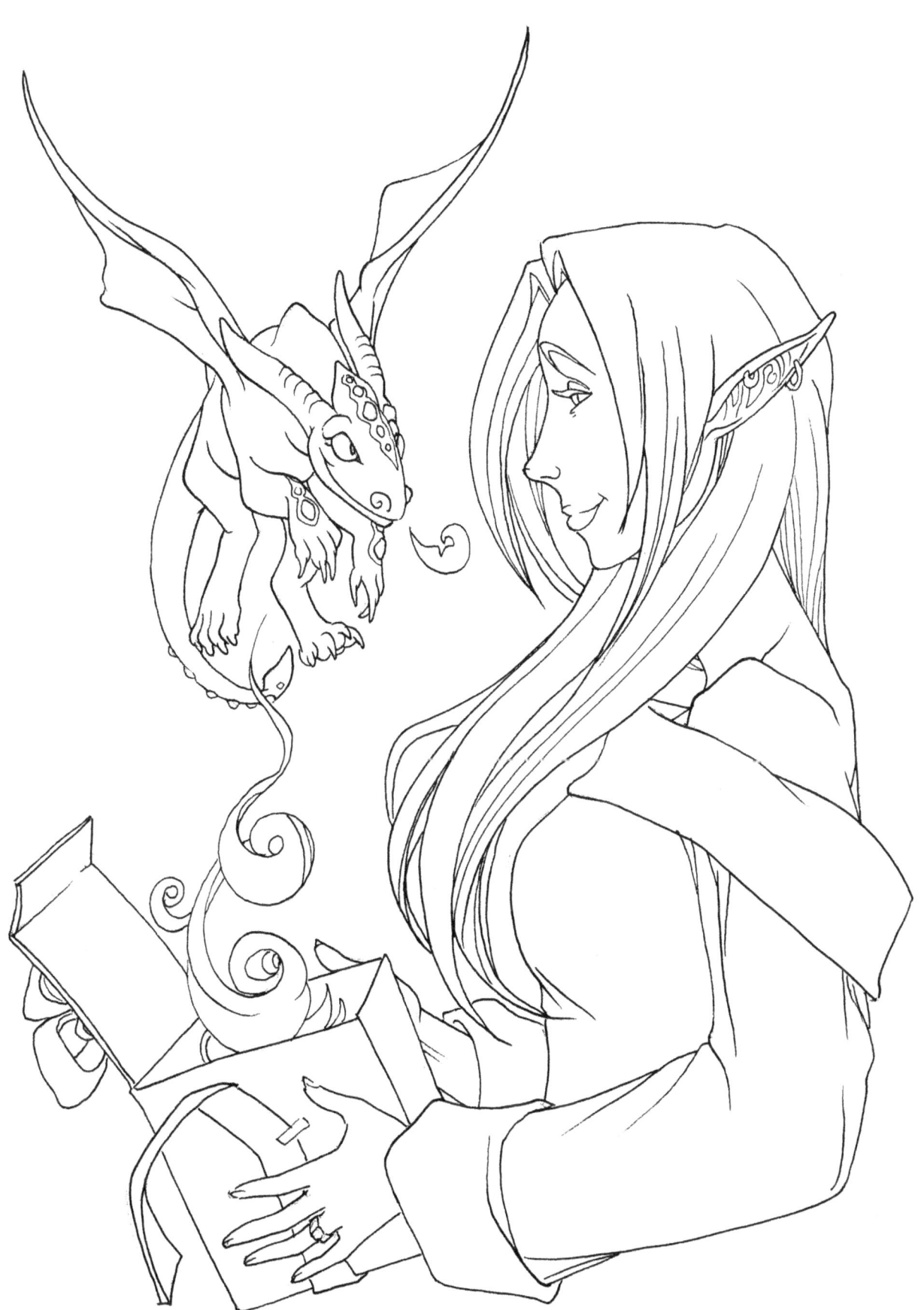

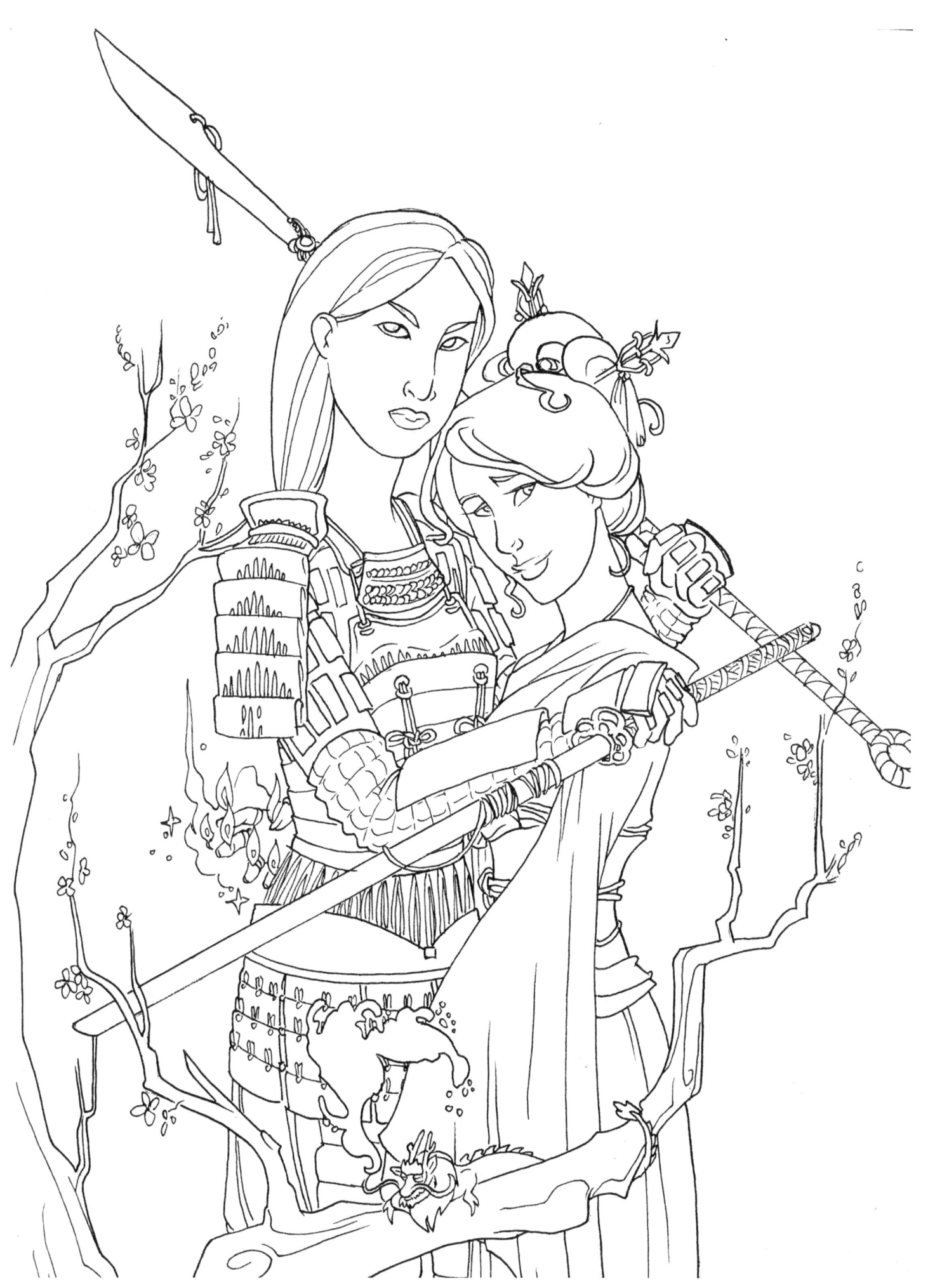

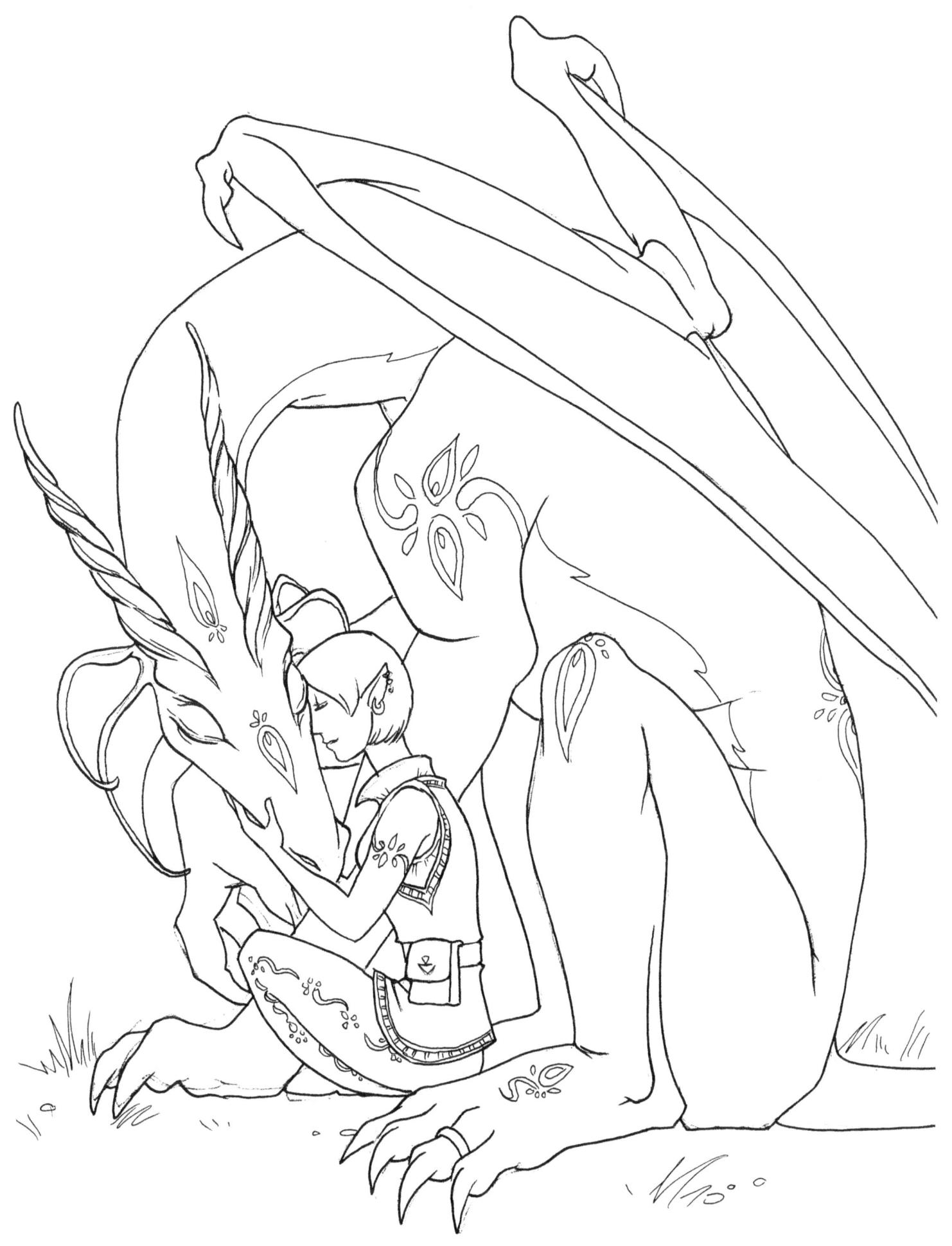

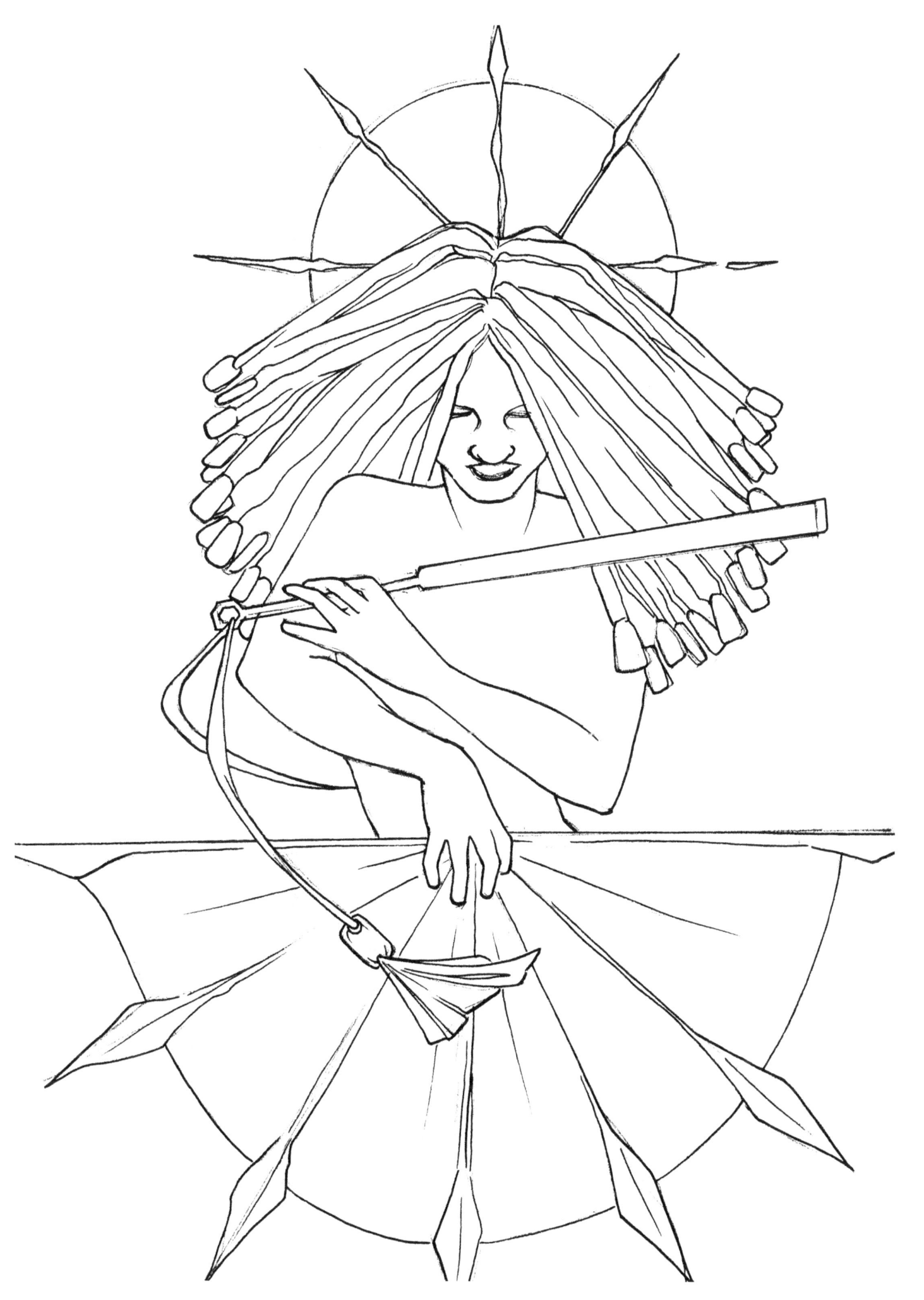

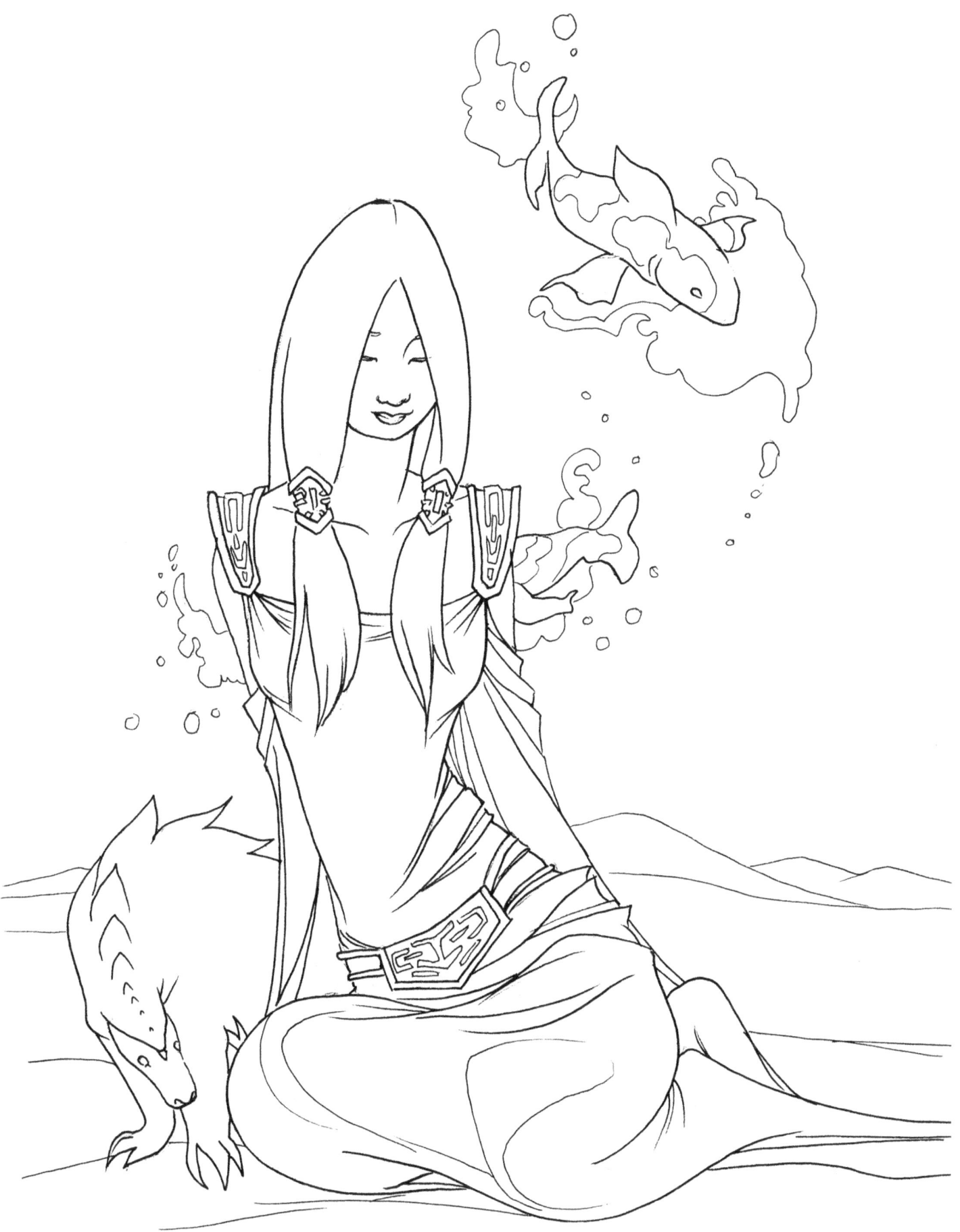

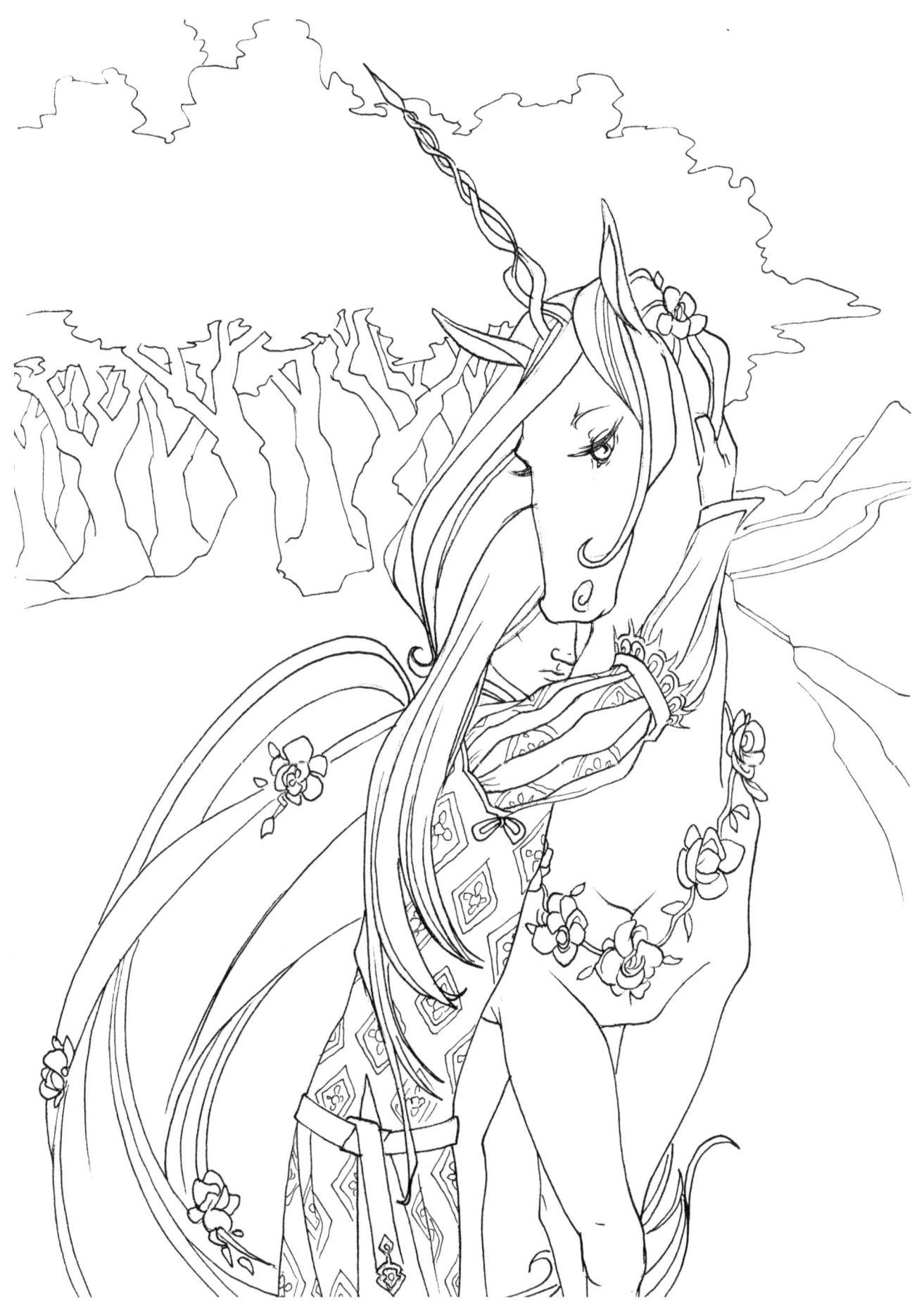

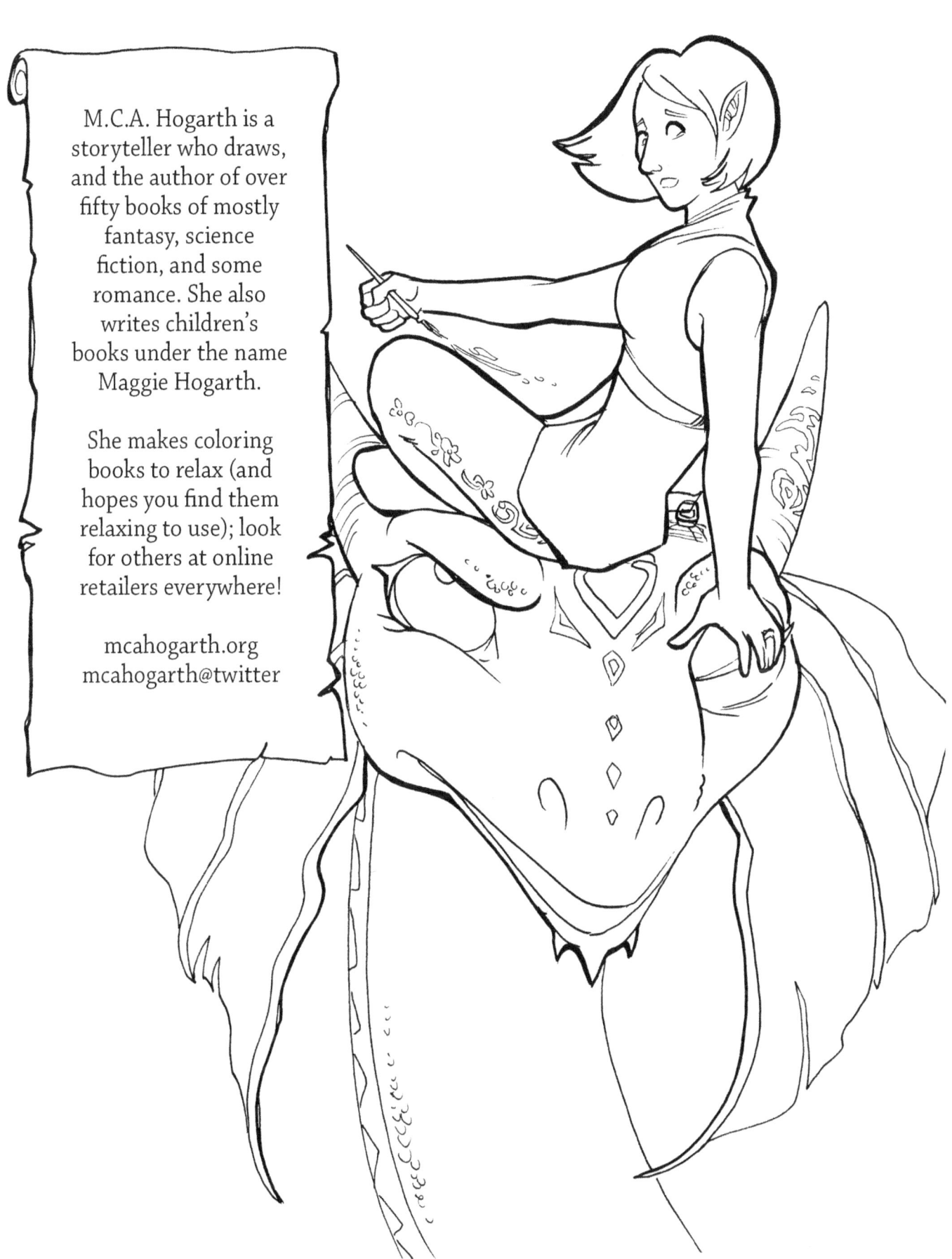

M.C.A. Hogarth is a storyteller who draws, and the author of over fifty books of mostly fantasy, science fiction, and some romance. She also writes children's books under the name Maggie Hogarth.

She makes coloring books to relax (and hopes you find them relaxing to use); look for others at online retailers everywhere!

mcahogarth.org
mcahogarth@twitter

www.ingramcontent.com/pod-product-compliance
Lightning Source LLC
Chambersburg PA
CBHW081241170526
45165CB00009B/3146